56 ARCHEOLOGY
57 ARCTIC & ANTARCTIC
58 BUILDING
59 PIRATE
60 NORTH AMERICAN INDIAN
AFRICA
OCEAN

63 BATTLE
64 GORILLA, MONKEY & APE
65 MEDIEVAL LIFE
66 FARM
67 SPY
68 RELIGION
69 EAGLE & BIRDS OF PREY

70 WITCHES & MAGIC-MAKERS
71 SPACE EXPLORATION
72 SHIPWRECK
73 CRIME & DETECTION
74 RUSSIA
75 LIGHT
76 ENERGY

77 ELECTRICITY
78 FORCE & MOTION
79 CHEMISTRY
80 MATTER
81 TIME & SPACE
82 ASTRONOMY
83 EARTH

84 LIFE
85 EVOLUTION
86 ECOLOGY
87 HUMAN BODY
88 MEDICINE
89 TECHNOLOGY
90 ELECTRONICS

91 RENAISSANCE
92 IMPRESSIONISM
93 GOYA
94 MANET
95 MONET
96 VAN GOGH
97 WATERCOLOR

98 PERSPECTIVE
99 DANCE
100 FUTURE
101 MYTHOLOGY
102 LEONARDO & HIS TIMES
103 OLYMPICS
104 MEDIA & COMMUNICATION

105 TITANIC
106 FOOTBALL
107 HURRICANE & TORNADO
108 SOCCER
109 PRESIDENTS
110 BASEBALL

BIBLE
LANDS

Assyrian plaque showing winged goddess

Gold pendant, 16th century B.C.

Late Bronze Age pilgrim flask

Late Bronze Age necklace with carnelian beads

Jewish coins from the Roman period

Middle Bronze Age axhead

Pottery vessel in the shape of a bull

Ceremonial baton from Ur

Gold earrings from
the Roman period

DK EYEWITNESS BOOKS

BIBLE LANDS

Bronze
and gold
toggle pins

Written by

JONATHAN N. TUBB

Assyrian
lion
carving

Ivory plaque
from Nimrud,
8th century B.C.

Phoenician
glass
vessels

Ivory carved
head, 13th
century B.C.

Dorling Kindersley

Ivory duck's head
found at Lachish

Bronze lamp
from Roman
period

Frieze showing Persian palace guard

Egyptian-style seal

DK

Dorling Kindersley

LONDON, NEW YORK, AUCKLAND, DELHI, JOHANNESBURG,
MUNICH, PARIS and SYDNEY

For a full catalog, visit

DK www.dk.com

Project editor Phil Wilkinson
Art editor Martin Atcherley
Senior editor Helen Parker
Senior art editor Julia Harris
Production Louise Barratt
Picture research Diana Morris
Special photography Alan Hills and Barbara Winter
of the British Museum, and Karl Shone

This Eyewitness ® Book has been conceived by
Dorling Kindersley Limited and Editions Gallimard

© 1991 Dorling Kindersley Limited
This edition © 2000 Dorling Kindersley Limited
First American edition, 1991

Published in the United States by Dorling Kindersley Publishing, Inc.
95 Madison Avenue, New York, NY 10016
2 4 6 8 10 9 7 5 3 1

Dorling Kindersley books are available at special discounts for bulk purchases for sales promotions or
premiums. Special editions, including personalized covers, excerpts of existing guides, and corporate
imprints can be created in large quantities for specific needs. For more information, contact Special
Markets Dept., Dorling Kindersley Publishing, Inc., 95 Madison Ave., New York,
NY 10016; Fax: (800) 600-9098

Library of Congress Cataloging-in-Publication Data
Tubb, Jonathan N.
Bible Lands / written by Jonathan Tubb.
p. cm. — (Eyewitness Books) Includes index.
Summary: Photographs and text document life in Biblical times, surveying the clothing, food, and
civilizations of a wide variety of cultures, including the Israelites, Babylonians,
Persians, and Romans.
1. Bible—Antiquities—Juvenile literature. 2. Bible—History of contemporary events—Juvenile
literature. 3. Middle East—Antiquities—Juvenile literature.
[1. Bible—Antiquities. 2. Middle East—Civilization—To 622.] I. Title. II. Series.
BS621.T83 2000 220.9'1—dc20 91-2388
ISBN 0-7894-5771-7 (pb)   ISBN 0-7894-5770-9 (hc)
Color reproduction by Colourscan, Singapore
Printed in China by Toppan Printing Co. (Shenzhen) Ltd.

Carved ivory found at Nimrud

Persian
silver stag

Persian
silver bowl

Selection of
arrowheads

Contents

Ivory carving showing winged sphinx

Lands of the Bible

T HE HOLY LAND is a region of great diversity. From west to east four different kinds of terrain are found. The coastal plain is low-lying and dry in the south, narrowing to the north with stretches of marsh and lagoon. The second zone is the hill country behind the coast, well watered and fertile on the west-facing slopes and rising to rock ridges that form the spine of the hill country. The third zone, the Jordan Valley, is almost rainless. The highlands of Jordan and the plateau beyond make up the fourth zone. There are rugged mountains in the south of the highlands and rolling hills to the north. The plateau is made up of farmland, giving way to dry steppe country (treeless plains) and finally desert.

Landscape near the Dead Sea

By the Dead Sea, looking east to the hills of Moab

Village of Dir-Zamet, near Hebron

MOUNT HERMON

Dan • LAKE HULEH

Hazor • Capernaum • SEA OF GALILEE

GILEAD

JORDAN RIVER Tell es-Sa'idiyeh •

Tiwal esh-Sharqi •

• Tiberias

Beth shan •

UPPER GALILEE

LOWER GALILEE

PLAIN OF PHOENICIA

Tirzah •

Nazareth •

Tyre •

Megiddo •

Samaria •

Acre •

Caesarea •

MEDITERRANEAN SEA

"Lot's wife" – a pillar of rock near the Dead Sea

THE BIBLE LANDS
The Holy Land, also referred to at different times in its history as Palestine and Canaan, lies in the Levant (the eastern Mediterranean). This map shows some of the most important places mentioned in this book, together with the seas and lakes and the River Jordan. North is to the left-hand side of the map.

View of Jerusalem by Carl Werner (1809-94)

Mount Sinai, south of the map area, was the scene of many of the Old Testament stories

Landscape by the Sea of Galilee

MOAB

EDOM

Qumran

DEAD SEA

Jericho

Masada

Herodium

Jerusalem
Bethlehem

JUDEAN HILLS

Hebron

NEGEV

Lachish

Beer-sheba

Ashdod

PLAIN OF PHILISTIA

Gaza

Modern fishing boats on the Sea of Galilee

CHRONOLOGY OF THE BIBLE LANDS	
Paleolithic (Old Stone Age)	700,000-15,000 B.C.
Mesolithic (Middle Stone Age)	15,000-8,300 B.C.
Neolithic (New Stone Age)	8,300-4,500 B.C.
Chalcolithic	4500-3200 B.C.
Early Bronze Age	3200-2000 B.C.
Middle Bronze Age	2000-1550 B.C.
Late Bronze Age	1550-1150 B.C.
Iron Age	1200-586 B.C.
Babylonian and Persian Periods	586-332 B.C.
Hellenistic Period	332-37 B.C.
Roman Period	37 B.C.-A.D. 324
Byzantine Period	A.D. 324-640
Early Arab Period	A.D. 640-1099

Early ancestors

MUCH OF OUR KNOWLEDGE of the early prehistory of the Holy Land comes from the site of Jericho, near the northern end of the Red Sea. Here, excavations have uncovered a remarkable series of settlements dating back to about 10,000 B.C., when Middle Stone Age (Mesolithic) hunters settled there permanently. At first they built flimsy shelters of sticks and hides, but these were later replaced by houses built of sundried mud bricks. In settling down, these people took the all-important step which led in the end to cultivating crops and domesticating (taming and raising) animals – a process known as the "Neolithic revolution." Jericho was not alone. During the following 3,000 years small farming villages sprang up all over the area. During the New Stone Age (or Neolithic, 8300-4500 B.C.) stone, flint, and obsidian (a type of volcanic glass) were used for tools and weapons. The early, pre-pottery phase of the Neolithic is remarkable for its arts and crafts – weaving, basketry, carpentry, and sculpture. Pottery was first made in around 5500 B.C. Knowledge of copper working was acquired about 1,000 years later, during the period known as the Chalcolithic (from the Greek word for copper).

Painted eyes

FACE ART
In the Pre-pottery Neolithic period, people sometimes removed the skull from the skeleton of a dead person. The facial features were re-created in plaster, and hair was painted red or black. Ancestor worship may have been the reason for the sensitive treatment of such skulls. This example was found in Jericho.

FIRST CITY
In the Pre-pottery Neolithic period Jericho grew in a remarkable way. In contrast to the usual simple, unwalled villages, it became a real city, with massive walls and at least one large stone tower, seen here.

SCRAPER
Even after copper working began, flint tools continued to be used. One type is the "fan scraper," which might have been used for preparing animal skins for clothing.

STONY FACE
This finely carved limestone face mask dates to the Pre-pottery Neolithic period. It comes from er-Ram, near Jerusalem, Israel.

Fan scraper

Scraper

Pupils colored with bitumen

Eyeliner made with dioptase, a green pigment, or coloring substance

Dried bundled reeds

MAN OF STRAW
This is a reconstruction of the reed framework of one of the statues from 'Ain Ghazal. The plaster was built up on this framework until the artist had formed the required shape.

GODS OR ANCESTORS?
These extraordinary statues, the earliest sizable sculptures of the human form ever found, were modeled in lime plaster over frameworks of reed bundles. Dating to around 6800 B.C., they come from a group of some 25 similar figures found in 1983, crushed together in a pit at the Neolithic site of 'Ain Ghazal, Jordan. Whether they represent gods, worshipers, or revered ancestors is not clear, but their function was almost certainly religious.

Body made of plaster over straw framework

tched roof makes suary look like small ouse

HOUSE OF BONES
n the coastal region of Palestine during the Chalcolithic period people were often buried in clay chests or "ossuaries."

CORNET
This unusual cornet-shaped vessel may have been a drinking cup. It comes from the Chalcolithic site of Teleilat Ghassul, Jordan.

The patriarchs

ABRAHAM, ISAAC, JACOB, AND JOSEPH were the patriarchs of the book of Genesis. They are considered the "founding fathers" of what was to become Israel. Archeology has provided a wealth of information about the time in which their stories are set, and the cultures of the lands through which they are believed to have traveled. The patriarchal stories may have taken place between about 2600 and 1800 B.C., with the tales of Abraham being the earliest, those of Joseph in Egypt the latest. Traditionally Abraham is said to have gone from Ur in Iraq to the Holy Land, by way of Harran in Turkey. Although there is no archeological proof that this journey took place, there is little doubt that it could have been made.

A gold shell used as a cosmetic container, used in Ur about 4,000 years ago

PATRIARCHS' PATH
This map shows the areas between which the patriarchs traveled. They could have gone with trading caravans, or followed the Bedouin, learning the skills of nomadic life.

ROYAL RICHES
At the time of Abraham's departure from Ur, it was a prosperous city. Many of the graves excavated by Sir Leonard Woolley in the 1920s and 1930s were found to contain expensive gifts for the afterlife, such as this ceremonial baton ornamented with gold, lapis lazuli, and mother-of-pearl.

TEMPLE TOWER
One of the most important buildings at Ur was the ziggurat, a type of tower built of mud bricks, several stories high, with a temple on top. The biblical Tower of Babel (in the city of Babylon) would have been a similar structure.

GOLDEN GLO
An idea of
wealth of the ro
family of Ur can
gained from
objects found
their graves, su
as this fine go
drinking c

Simple bow

Lyre – remains of similar instruments found at Ur

Tunic made of colored and embroidered wool

Bellows, suggesting that some of the people were metalworkers

Duckbill ax (p. 45)

Donkey, one of the earliest beasts of burden

Women wear shoes, in contrast to the men's sandals

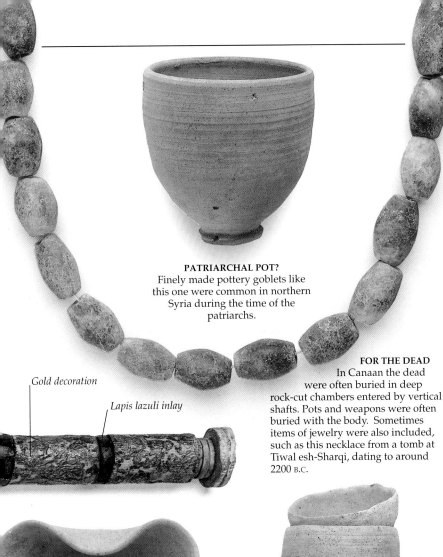

PATRIARCHAL POT?
Finely made pottery goblets like this one were common in northern Syria during the time of the patriarchs.

Gold decoration

Lapis lazuli inlay

FOR THE DEAD
In Canaan the dead were often buried in deep rock-cut chambers entered by vertical shafts. Pots and weapons were often buried with the body. Sometimes items of jewelry were also included, such as this necklace from a tomb at Tiwal esh-Sharqi, dating to around 2200 B.C.

DRINKER'S DELIGHT
This unusual flask from northern Syria was a device for raising liquid. Fluid entered through holes in the base and could be retained by clamping a thumb over the narrow mouth. The liquid could then be released by removing the thumb pressure.

FISHY FLAME
In the patriarchal period the people of Canaan used fish oil in their lamps. It gave such low light that four wicks were needed.

YOGURT MAKER
Yogurt (known as leben) has always been an important food in the eastern Mediterranean. This pair of vessels from Jordan is thought to have been used for making yogurt.

VISITORS FROM CANAAN
The stories of Joseph's adventures in Egypt are best set in the period 2000-1800 B.C., when archeological evidence has shown that Asiatic people were entering Egypt. These wall paintings are from the tomb of an Egyptian named Amenemhet at Beni Hasan. They show a group of Asiatics, probably Canaanites, being introduced to the Egyptian court.

Sickle sword

Woolen kilt

Group's leader is called Absha

Egypt

IN THE EARLY BRONZE AGE the opening of trade routes to Egypt allowed a thriving city-based economy to develop in Canaan. In the Middle Bronze Age, groups of Canaanites moved into northern Egypt and established a local dynasty called the Hyksos, who eventually took over the whole of Egypt. Only in the Late Bronze Age, in about 1550 B.C., did the Egyptian pharaohs expel the Hyksos, launch a military campaign against Canaan, and bring it under Egyptian control. Egypt imposed heavy taxes on Canaan, but in return the Canaanite cities gained security and better access to international markets. In the reign of Ramses II (1304-1237 B.C.), the empire was reorganized. Key strategic cities like Beth Shan and Gaza were strengthened, others were allowed to decline. Many people were made homeless and migrated to the Judean hill country, where they established small farming settlements. These dispossessed Canaanites, known to the Egyptians as Hapiru (or Hebrews), formed the basis of what was to become Israel.

EGYPT AND CANAA..
In the Late Bronze Age Canaa.. became part of the Egyptia.. Empire. Her local rulers becam.. vassals of the pharaoh. Some .. the cities of Canaan, like Gaz.. prospered under the Egyptian..

LOST AND FOUND
According to the Bible, Moses, leader of the Hebrew exodus (departure from Egypt), was found in the bulrushes.

POWER SYMBOL
This Egyptian ceremonial ax has an elaborate openwork head.

LETTER TO THE PHARAOH
The Armana letters contain reports from vassal rulers of the empire to Egyptian pharaoh Amenophis III. Some mention trouble caused by lawless bands of "Hapiru," homeless peoples living on the fringes of cities. The Hapiru are related to the biblical Hebrews.

STRONGHOLD
Beth Shan was one of the major centers of Egyptian control in Canaan. During the time of Ramses II, the city was occupied by Egyptian troops and had an Egyptian governor.

HEBREW SLAVES?
Both the Bible and an Egyptian papyrus refer to "Hapiru" employed as laborers in Ramses II's building projects. They may not actually have been slaves, as suggested in this detail of a painting by 19th-century artist Sir Edward Poynter.

The Philistines

In Ramses III's reign (1198-1166 B.C.), the Egyptian Empire faced a major crisis when it was invaded by a league of peoples from the Aegean (the Greek islands) and southern Anatolia (modern Turkey). Known as the sea peoples, they included a group called the Philistines. Ramses pushed them back from the shores of Egypt in a great naval battle. But he could not stop them from settling in Canaan, at the southern end of the coastal strip.

FINE FEATHERS
Philistine warriors wore feathered headdresses.

ILISTINE FACE
e Philistines, like some of the other sea peoples,
ried their dead in distinctive "slipper-shaped"
ffins. The lids show grotesquely modeled human
tures.

After Ramses II reorganized his empire the number of hill-farming settlements in Judea increased dramatically.

RTING OF THE WATERS
though archeology cannot confirm the
ry of the Hebrew exodus through
e waters of the Red Sea, it is not
likely that a group of "Hapiru"
t Egypt during the reign of
mses II and found their way
the Judean hill country.

SUCCESSFUL PHARAOH
Ramses II brought to an end Egypt's long conflict with the Hittites of Anatolia. After fighting the Hittites at the Battle of Kadesh in 1289 B.C., the Egyptians signed a treaty which brought them a period of peace and prosperity. Ramses II was most probably the pharaoh of the biblical exodus.

*Striped
headcloth
indicates
kingship*

Living on a mound

T HE PEOPLE OF the Middle and Late Bronze Ages in Palestine are traditionally known as the Canaanites. But the distinctive Canaanite culture did not appear fully formed at the beginning of this period: it developed gradually and its origins can be traced back to the 4th millennium B.C. By this time, the people of Egypt, Syria, and Mesopotamia had formed cities and developed systems of writing. The growth of trade routes led to similar developments in Palestine. Many of the small villages of the Chalcolithic period were abandoned. New groups of people entering the country around 3200 B.C. established themselves at new sites chosen for their natural resources and designed to benefit from the growing web of trade connections. Often, these sites would be settled for thousands of years afterward. As generation after generation lived and built upon the same spot, huge artificial mounds of debris (household rubbish and the foundations of old houses) built up. These mounds, still visible today, are known as tells.

Portrait of a Canaanite, a Late Bronze Age ivory from Lachish

Canaanite pottery of the Early Bronze Age, like this jug, is elegant and well made.

A "section," or vertical cross section through t. tell, revealing walls, floors, layers of ash and rubbish, pits, ovens, and other features that sho. the site's history of occupation

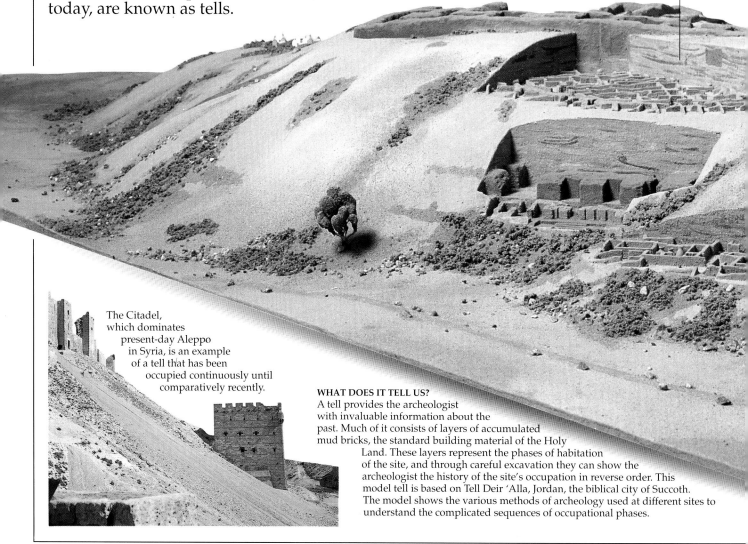

The Citadel, which dominates present-day Aleppo in Syria, is an example of a tell that has been occupied continuously until comparatively recently.

WHAT DOES IT TELL US?
A tell provides the archeologist with invaluable information about the past. Much of it consists of layers of accumulated mud bricks, the standard building material of the Holy Land. These layers represent the phases of habitation of the site, and through careful excavation they can show the archeologist the history of the site's occupation in reverse order. This model tell is based on Tell Deir 'Alla, Jordan, the biblical city of Succoth. The model shows the various methods of archeology used at different sites to understand the complicated sequences of occupational phases.

THE CITY OF LACHISH
This reconstruction of Lachish shows the tell as it might have been at the time of the siege in 701 B.C. (p. 46). The two walls are clearly visible, as is the strongly fortified gateway.

OUNTING DEFENSES
y the time of the Middle
ronze Age many of the major
ll sites had risen to
nsiderable heights and were
coming unstable around the
dges. So the inhabitants
rengthened the sides and
dded a coat of plaster to
em. This created a smooth
ope called a "glacis," which
rovided a good defensive
arrier. At the top of the glacis
tall defensive rampart was
ade, which was crowned by
e city wall itself. The base of
e glacis was held in by a
rong retaining wall, and a
tch (or"fosse") around the
ase of the mound completed the defenses.
laborate gateways, like the one at Tell Dan,
orthern Israel, were built into the walls.

EXPENSIVE TASTES
The Canaanites liked to have attractive things around them. This jar, made of faience (p. 37), was found at Lachish. It was imported from Egypt.

Ledge handles typical of Canaanite pottery of this period

POURER
The highly burnished finish of this pot is called "red slip," a popular surface treatment for Early Bronze Age tableware. The vessel has a spout for pouring and typical ledge handles.

Mud brick buildings, often difficult to distinguish from surrounding soil

Houses with wall paintings

The Canaanites

THE LAND OF CANAAN
We do not know exactly how Palestine was structured politically during the Middle Bronze Age. It was probably made up of a large number of independent city states, each ruled by a prince. Each city would have controlled its own area of land containing a number of dependent towns and villages.

THE FULL FLOWERING of Canaanite culture came in the Middle Bronze Age (c. 2000-1550 B.C.). During this period Canaan was largely free of the power struggles and foreign interventions that were to dominate its later history. In this climate, the country developed an ever-expanding trade network. There was extensive trade with Egypt, and contacts were strengthened with Syria, Anatolia, and Cyprus. Canaan's art, architecture, and craftsmanship reached new levels of skill and sophistication as her artists were influenced by a variety of sources and countries. During the Late Bronze Age (1550-1150 B.C.) Canaan was dominated by Egypt. The Egyptian empire brought with it even more far-reaching trade links, including those with the Mycenaean people of mainland Greece. But the local culture, by now well established, continued to flourish.

STAR ATTRACTION
This finely made star pendant from Tell el-'Ajjul shows the skill of the Canaanite goldsmiths of the 16th century B.C.

POTS AND PALMS
Canaanite pots of the Late Bronze Age are often decorated with this design of palm trees and ibexes. The palm tree on this goblet from Lachish is highly stylized.

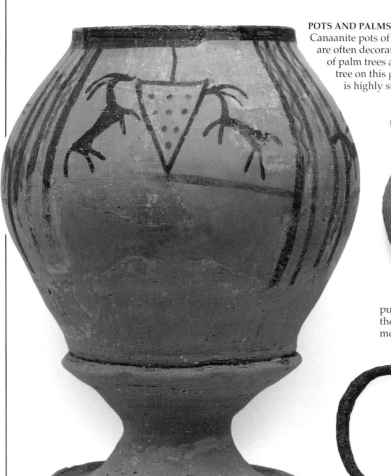

LITTLE DIPPER
"Dippers" were little jugs used to take liquid out of a larger container. People would often push a stick through the handle of the dipper and hang it over the mouth of the container.

PILGRIM'S PLEASURE
The Canaanites were very inventive. This amusing pilgrim flask, dating to the end of the Late Bronze Age, has its own built-in drinking cup.

SEAL OF APPROVAL
Egyptian-style seals and scarabs (seals in the shape of a beetle), used to denote ownership, were common in Canaan. Many were made by Canaanite craftsmen, and some were exported to Egypt.

King riding on chariot

King seated on throne decorated with sphinxes

KINGLY SPLENDOR
A superbly carved ivory plaque from Megiddo gives a rare glimpse of the Canaanite royal court. It shows the king, seated on a throne supported by sphinxes, receiving a victory procession. The king is also shown in his chariot.

BULL MARKET
This vessel in the shape of a bull was imported to Canaan from Cyprus.

FOREIGN FLOWERS
Egyptian influence was very strong toward the end of the Late Bronze Age. This necklace from Tell es-Sa'idiyeh has beads made of carnelian in the shape of Egyptian lotus flower seed pods.

A LEG TO STAND ON
Small bronze figures were often made as temple offerings. This one from Lachish represents a disabled Canaanite who has lost the lower part of his left leg. (The broken arm is accidental.)

CITY MOUND
The sites of many Canaanite city mounds or tells (pp. 14-15) are still clear in today's landscape in the Holy Land.

WHOSE HEAD?
Dating to the 13th century B.C., this head from Lachish shows strongly Egyptian features. It was probably made as a piece of decorative inlay, perhaps to adorn the arm of a chair.

Carnelian bead

COSTLY IMPORT
During the Late Bronze Age, high-quality pottery was imported to Canaan from Mycenae. Many such pots are thought to have contained expensive perfumed oils.

Death and burial

ANCIENT PEOPLE made efforts to treat their dead with great care. In the Holy Land this often involved creating elaborate graves, sometimes dug deeply into the natural rock. Burial, rather than cremation, was the usual practice, and a belief in the afterlife is shown from the earliest periods – not only from the religious writings of historical times but also from the evidence of the graves themselves. From the earliest times the deceased was accompanied with grave goods (items needed for the afterlife), such as jewelry, pottery, tools, and weapons. Food and drink were also included. Excavating such burials gives the archeologist a rich source of information about the people themselves – their beliefs, the objects they used and cherished, their physical characteristics, and even the diseases that afflicted them. The objects shown here come from a child's grave excavated at Tell es-Sa'idiyeh, Jordan, the biblical city of Zarethan.

FASTENE
This pin, found near the le shoulder of the skeleto would have fastened t shroud in which th child was burie

BRIGHT BRACELET
The girl wore a bracelet of carnelian and silver beads on her left wrist.

A silver finger ring was worn on the left hand

LUCKY CHARM?
A simple ring carved out of steatite (soapstone) was found, not on the girl's finger, but on top of her chest. It may originally have been held on a string around her neck.

ONE BY ONE
Earrings, like this silver one, were often worn singly. This one, found beneath the skull, w probably worn on the left e

FINE DECORATION
Bronze bangles were worn as jewelry throughout the Iron Age. This pair have delicate engraved decorations. They were worn as anklets.

ON THE HEAD
This unusual clasp was found placed on top of the skull. It may have been fixed to a cap, perhaps to attach a tassel.

Incised decoration on terminal (end) of bangle

Grooves to hold thread

THE ANKLETS IN POSITION
This detail of the girl's lower legs show the bronze anklets in the position in which they were found.

NERY
...e girl buried in this grave clearly
...me from a wealthy family. Her
...autiful necklace is made of
...ernating silver and carnelian
...ads with a central group made of
...ate. The silver beads are finely
...orked.

...ver beads are
...gmented and
...ely granulated
...43)

Strainer

Spout

JUST FOR FUN?
This finely decorated
bronze spindle is an
unusual burial gift. Perhaps
spinning was one of the child's
favorite pastimes.

FEEDING BOTTLE
This pot in the shape of an animal
(perhaps a calf) is the most moving item
in the grave. It has a strainer in the top
and a hole through the snout, and may
have been a feeding bottle. It was slightly
broken when put into the grave and was
probably much loved – somewhat like a
teddy bear with a missing ear.

SIMPLE SHELLS
A bracelet of tiny white shell
beads was worn on the girl's
right wrist.

A young girl's burial

...he objects on this page come from
...e grave of a seven-year-old girl.
...he was buried in a simple pit, and
...aces of a white substance in the
...oil showed that her body was
...rapped in a fine linen shroud. This
...hotograph, taken at the end of the
excavation, shows
many of the grave
goods in position.

MARK OF STATUS
The child's seal shows a
bull and a winged symbol
representing the sun.
Again, the inclusion of a
seal shows the high status
of the girl's family.

19

The Israelites

Delicate ivory furniture ornament from Samaria

B<small>Y</small> ABOUT 1150 B.C., the Egyptians had effectively withdrawn from Canaan, leaving a vacuum to be filled by the Israelites and the Philistines. For nearly 100 years they lived side by side, the Philistines on the coastal plain, the Israelites in the more barren hill country. But during the 11th century B.C., the Philistines tried to extend their territory. Faced with this threat, the Israelites united into one nation under the leadership of first Saul, then David. In about 1000 B.C. David captured Jerusalem and was proclaimed king of the Israelite nation. He finally defeated the Philistines and expanded Israel's territory. The kingdom continued to flourish under David's son Solomon, who extended Israel's trading network and built the Great Temple in Jerusalem. After Solomon's death in 928 B.C., tensions between the north and south of the kingdom came to a head. The monarchy finally split in two. The capital of Judah, in the south, was Jerusalem; Israel, in the north, had its capital at Samaria.

NO SMOKE WITHOUT FIRE
This lively 19th-century engraving represents the destruction of the Temple by the Babylonians in 587 B.C.

THE TWO KINGDOMS
This map shows the area of David's kingdom, which divided into two: Israel in the north and Judah in the south.

FIRST MENTION OF ISRAEL
This stela (stone marker) of the pharaoh Merneptah (1235-1223 B.C.) records a military campaign in Canaan directed against Gezer, Ashkelon, and Israel. This is the first recorded mention of Israel as a political unit, representing the farming communities of the Judean hill country.

BOTTOMS UP
Probably a furniture ornament, this ivory fragment from King Ahab's palace at Samaria shows the hindquarters of a lion. Relations between Israel and Phoenicia (pp. 22-23) were close, and Phoenician artisans were often used for fine work such as this.

Porch

Bronze columns called Jachin and Boaz

Solomon's Temple

Wealth from trade, and a good central administration, enabled Solomon to carry out large-scale building projects. Impressive public buildings, gateways, and city walls were built at several major sites. The most important project was the Temple in Jerusalem. No traces of the building can be seen now, but there are detailed descriptions of it in the Bible. This evidence, together with excavations at other sites, has made possible various reconstructions of the Temple like the one shown here.

Solomon

hall lined
cedar

SPHINXES OR CHERUBIM?
The "cherubim," often mentioned in the Bible, were winged sphinxes (human-headed lions).

Holy of Holies, paneled with cedar and inlaid with gold

"Cherubim" (sphinxes)

This elegant Israelite decanter, used for serving wine or water, is from 8th-century Judah.

Raised platform

KING'S MARK
The Judean royal winged scarab symbol, together with the name "Socoh," are stamped on this jar handle. Socoh was one of four administrative centers for the distribution of items such as grain, wine, and oil.

AN ARMY OF WORKERS
This imaginative 19th-century view shows the building of Solomon's Temple.

The Phoenicians

The Phoenician writing on this seal identifies its owner as "Tamak-el, son of Milkam"

B<small>Y THE SECOND MILLENNIUM</small> B.C. the Israelites occupied most of Palestine except for the southern coastal strip, which was held by the Philistines. To the north, the powerful Aramean kingdoms controlled most of central and northern Syria. The remaining Canaanite territory, in the northwest, became Phoenicia. The name derives from the Greek word for "purple," because the Phoenician cities were well known for their technique of purple fabric dyeing (p. 41). There was little farming land in Phoenicia, so the people turned to the sea to make a living, becoming great seafarers and traders. The Phoenicians were also excellent craft workers, and their work was in demand all over the Middle East. Solomon is said to have employed Phoenician workers to build his temple in Jerusalem.

THE LAND OF THE PHOENICIANS
The Phoenicians were based mainly in the cities of Byblos, Sidon, and Tyre, in the coastal area shaded in red on the map.

MUCH-TRAVELED POT
This elegant painted jug was probably used for perfumed oil. Vessels like this were traded widely throughout the eastern Mediterranean.

Sphinx

Geometric design

MIXED MOTIFS *above*
The much-traveled Phoenicians produced art that blended together a variety of styles or motifs. This bronze bowl combines Egyptian sphinxes with northern Syrian geometric designs. The overall arrangement is more typical of the Aegean.

FAST MOVER
This Assyrian relief shows a Phoenician ship. It is a bireme, a ship with two banks of oars on each side. Doubling up the oars made the ship fast and effective.

TRADING POST
The Phoenicians are best known as seafarers. Their merchants traveled far from their homeland and set up colonies around the Mediterranean. The most famous was Carthage, in northern Africa, founded in 814 B.C. by settlers from Tyre.

PRECIOUS BOOTY
This piece of carved ivory was used to decorate an item of furniture. It was found at Nimrud, the Assyrian capital, and was probably brought there as tribute (p. 48) or booty from a military campaign.

BRITTLE BUT BEAUTIFUL
Glassmaking was one of the most important industries of the Phoenician cities. A paste of finely ground sand mixed with soda was used, and various pigments were added. When fired at a high temperature, the mixture fused to form colored glass.

SHAPING UP
Glassblowing had not been invented in Phoenician times, so vessels like this were made by molding the glass paste around a clay core.

Shields

PORT OF CALL
The Phoenicians carried out major engineering projects to transform existing natural harbors into large ports capable of handling the international shipping on which their cities depended. This is a modern view of Byblos, one of their ports.

Double ranks of oars

Inscription reads "Arrowhead of 'Ada,' son of Ba'l'a'"

AS EASY AS ABC
The Canaanites probably invented the first alphabet in the Middle Bronze Age. But the Phoenicians refined and developed the system and some of their letters appear on this arrowhead. Their 22-letter alphabet formed the basis of the Greek and ultimately the Roman alphabets.

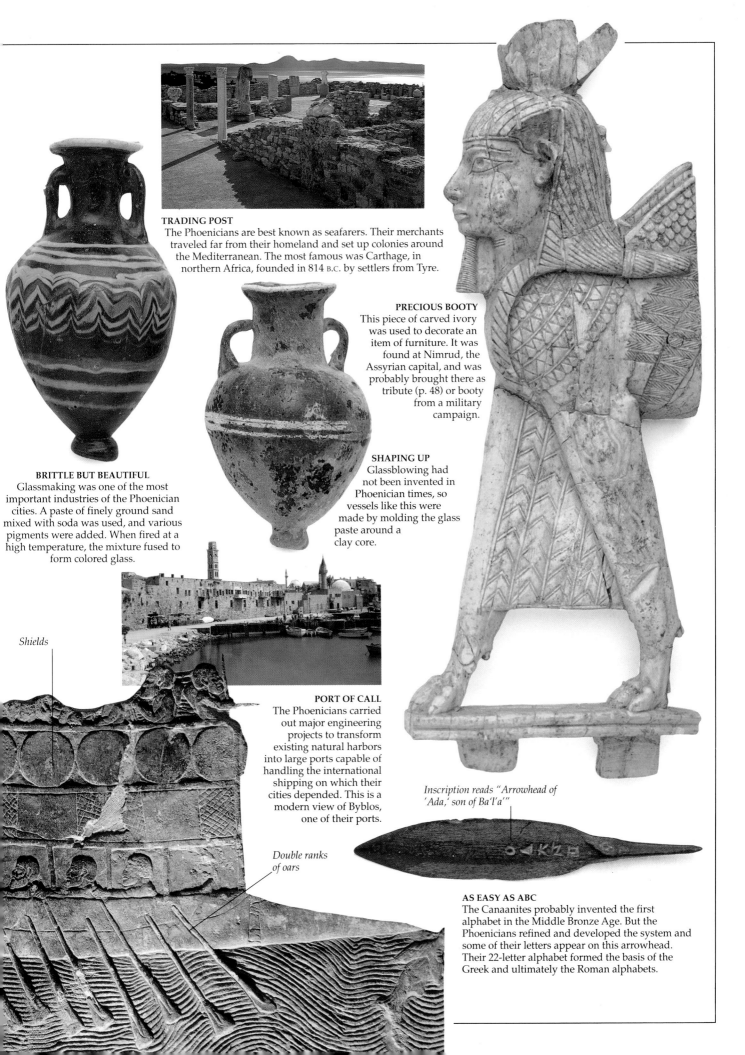

Gods and goddesses

Until the israelite concept of the "One God" was widely accepted, religion in the Holy Land involved the worship of a variety of gods and goddesses. These gods were thought to dominate every aspect of life – war, weather, fertility, the harvest, and so on. Most of what we know about them comes from a large archive of clay tablets, dating to the Late Bronze Age, found at the site of Ras Shamra, Syria. The tablets tell of the supreme god, El, the "father of man," whose domain was the heavens. His wife, Asherah, ruled over the seas. Their children made up a group of over 70 other deities (gods) including the storm and warrior god, Baal, and the goddess of love and fertility, Astarte.

EARLY GOD?
The lime-plaster statues from 'Ain Ghazal (p. 9) probably served some ritual function, but whether they were meant to represent gods or their worshipers is unknown.

FERTILITY FIGURE
Astarte, the Canaanite goddess of fertility, is depicted on this gold plaque. It comes from a hoard of goldwork found at Tell el-'Ajjul, dating to the 16th century B.C.

WARRIOR GOD
This bronze figure, ornamented with silver, dates to the Late Bronze Age. It is thought to represent the god Baal, who is depicted as a warrior, brandishing his weapon.

POPULAR DEITY
Perhaps the most powerful and popular Canaanite goddess, Astarte is usually shown naked, with her hands cupping her breasts. This plaque of Astarte is made of terra-cotta.

BAAL'S PROPHETS
King Ahab married Jezebel, a Phoenician princess who reestablished worship of the god Baal in Israel. The prophet Elijah called upon God to light a sacrificial fire in front of the prophets of Baal, to show His superiority.

BY THE LIGHT OF THE MOON
This Canaanite temple, excavated at Hazor, was dedicated to the worship of the moon god and his wife.

EGYPTIAN EY
The eye of Horus was one of the mo popular Egyptian amulets (charms Representing the god Horus in both huma and falcon form, it combines a human ey with a falcon's feathe

WHOSE HAND?
Although many Canaanite temples and shrines have been excavated throughout Palestine, we do not usually know which gods and goddesses were worshiped in them. This finely carved ivory hand was all that remained of a statue from the "fosse" temple at Lachish (p. 37).

GOD OF WINE
This bust of the Nabatean (Arab) vine god Dushara is from the temple of Dushara at Si'a in the Hauran, southern Syria. It is carved in black basalt, a very hard local stone.

The facade of the Temple at Jerusalem depicted on a coin of Simon Bar Kochba, leader of the second Jewish revolt (p. 39)

ASTARTE LIVES ON
Despite Israelite religious laws prohibiting the worship of other gods and goddesses, models of Canaanite fertility goddesses, such as Astarte, continued to be produced throughout the Iron Age.

GODS OF EGYPT *left*
The gods of conquering powers were often worshiped alongside the Canaanite gods. Egyptian amulets appeared in the Late Bronze Age, when Canaan was ruled by Egypt; they remained popular in the Iron Age. These 9th-century B.C. amulets show the sphinx, with a cat's body and a woman's head, and Sekhmet, goddess of the burning heat of the sun.

Sekhmet   Sekhmet   Sphinx   Sekhmet

GODS OF GREECE
The Greek domination of Syria and Palestine after 332 B.C. brought with it the Greek religion and its gods and goddesses. Many of these became equated with traditional deities – for example, the Greek goddess Aphrodite took on the role of Astarte.

Food and crops

Mortar and pestle from the Iron Age

P ERHAPS THE MOST IMPORTANT advance made by early people was the development of agriculture. It enabled people to settle permanently in one place and to produce more food than they could eat, which in turn stimulated trade and population growth. In the Holy Land, this happened between about 9000 and 6000 B.C., during the final phase of the Stone Age. The process began with the selection of plants and animals that were suitable for cultivation and rearing. Then these species were bred selectively over hundreds of years, gradually becoming suited to the needs of humans. Early farmers grew two species of wheat, emmer and einkorn, and also barley. All three crops are native to the eastern Mediterranean. In addition to these cereals, a variety of fruits and vegetables were cultivated.

MILK AND HONEY
Moses' Canaan was indeed a land of "milk and honey," a fertile place with a long history of agriculture and horticulture (cultivation of vegetables and plants).

FROM THE PHARMACY
Herbs such as cumin were grown not only as flavorings but also for their medicinal value. Cumin was used to treat convulsions. Its oil was also used in perfume.

FAVORED FOR FLAVOR
The Book of Numbers records how the Israelites of the Exodus remembered with longing the fruits and vegetables they had left behind in Egypt. These included leeks, onions, and garlic. There is every reason to suppose that they would have found these growing in abundance in Canaan, too. Even today they are essential in Arabic cooking and are valued for their distinctive flavorings.

Spring onions

THE VERSATILE LENTIL
Lentils were grown from at least the 7th millennium B.C. They could be used in soups, pastes, and purées, or they could be combined with grains and ground into flour to make cakes.

Leeks

26

BLOWING IN THE WIND

After harvested cereals had been threshed (beaten to separate out the grains), they were tossed in the air, allowing the lighter chaff to blow away, leaving the heavy grains behind. This process is called "winnowing."

ON THE TERRACES

Terrace agriculture, common in the Holy Land is a way of growing crops on hillside sites.

FOR FOOD AND DRINK

Barley was one of the earliest cereals to be cultivated. It was used for making bread and brewing beer.

EARLY CROP

Although millet was widely cultivated in Mesopotamia from at least 3000 B.C., it does not seem to have been an important cereal crop in the Holy Land until post-Roman times.

WORKING WITH WHEAT

The grains of the earliest varieties of cultivated wheat, emmer and einkorn were covered by a tough sheath that was difficult to remove by threshing. By Biblical times, these cereals had been replaced as the main field crop by durum wheat. Durum, with its naked grains, was easy to thresh. It also made excellent flour for bread.

Cutting edge

CUTTER

During the first millennium B.C., sickles made of iron came into common usage.

GETTING IN THE HARVEST

Flint blades were set in wooden or bone handles to make sickles for harvesting cereal crops. They often had toothed edges. Developed in the Stone Age, such sickles were used well into the Bronze Age.

Continued on next page

Continued from previous page

THROUGH THE GROVES

This relief from the palace of the Assyrian king Sennacherib at Nineveh shows a group of Mesopotamian prisoners being led through the palm groves of southern Iraq.

THE GARDEN OF EDEN

The story of the Garden of Eden is illustrated in this painting by Roelandt Jacobsz Savery (1576-1639). The rich variety of the natural world, and the importance of humankind's relationship with the animals and plants, is demonstrated by the story.

FOREIGN FRUIT

In the early days of agriculture, fruit trees were often introduced from neighboring countries. Apples were probably brought to the Holy Land from Syria or Turkey around 4000 B.C.

SPICE OF LIFE

The Old Testament contains many references to spices. Joseph is said to have been sold by his brothers to Ishmaelite spice-merchants bound for Egypt. Cinnamon, used in cooking and flavoring wine, was imported from India.

MAJOR EXPORT

The olive tree, native to the Syria-Palestine region, became one of its most important natural resources. Olive oil was used in cooking, in medicine, as a base for perfumes, and as a fuel for lamps. It became a major export and was being produced on an industrial scale by the Bronze Age.

Fresh figs

EARLY FRUIT

It is not known where the fig was first cultivated but it was well established in the Holy Land by about 5000 B.C.

Dried figs

Compressed dried figs

STANDBY

Figs were often eaten fresh, but they could also be dried. In this form they could be kept for months, providing a useful reserve food supply in times when other foods were scarce.

OIL SPILLAGE

Olive oil was usually kept in large storage jars. But it would have been served at the table in small juglets, like this one from Tell es-Sa'idiyeh, dating to the 12th century B.C.

POCKET SNACK

Figs could be pressed and made into cakes. Such cakes formed an ideal source of highly nutritious food for long journeys. Perhaps Abraham carried fig cakes on his journey to Canaan from Ur (p. 12).

PRIZED SPECIMEN
The acacia tree is one of the few to grow in the Sinai desert. Acacia wood was used for the Ark of the Covenant described in the biblical Book of Exodus.

POPULAR PROTEINS
Nuts are easily gathered and stored for long periods. The most popular were pistachios and almonds; these are the only two mentioned in the Bible. The pistachio, native to Syria, was widely cultivated.

Pistachios

DATE HARVEST
This relief comes from Tell Halaf (ancient Gozan) in Syria and dates to the 9th century B.C. It shows a man using a ladder to gather dates.

Almonds

PRECIOUS POMEGRANATE
This fruit was prized for its bittersweet juice. Its original homes were in Asia Minor, the Caucasus, Armenia, and Persia, but it was certainly established in the Holy Land by the Middle Bronze Age. Examples of the carbonized fruit were found in a tomb at Jericho dating to this period.

The olive seems to have been cultivated from at least 4000 B.C., not only for its delicious fruit but also for its highly prized oil.

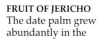

FRUIT OF JERICHO
The date palm grew abundantly in the Fertile Crescent, the area stretching from Egypt and the Holy Land around to the northern end of the Persian Gulf. It provided a mainstay of the diet of early people in the area. Jericho is referred to in the Old Testament as the "city of palm trees." The Jericho date was a well-known variety, valued for its juiciness.

Continued on next page

Continued from previous page

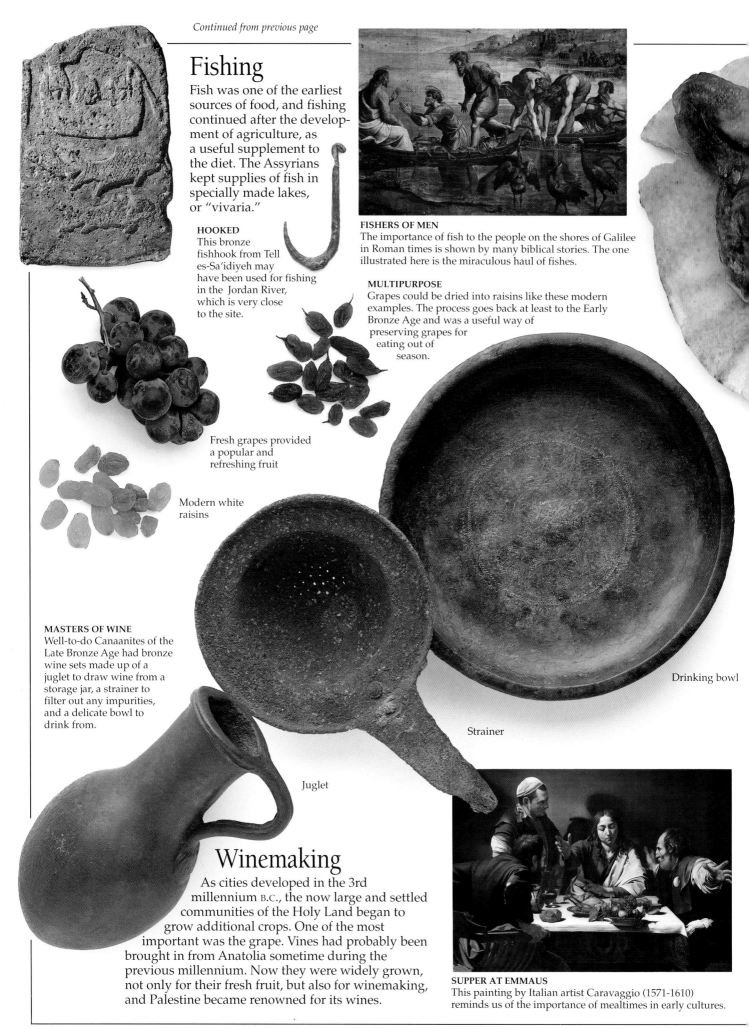

Fishing

Fish was one of the earliest sources of food, and fishing continued after the development of agriculture, as a useful supplement to the diet. The Assyrians kept supplies of fish in specially made lakes, or "vivaria."

HOOKED
This bronze fishhook from Tell es-Sa'idiyeh may have been used for fishing in the Jordan River, which is very close to the site.

FISHERS OF MEN
The importance of fish to the people on the shores of Galilee in Roman times is shown by many biblical stories. The one illustrated here is the miraculous haul of fishes.

MULTIPURPOSE
Grapes could be dried into raisins like these modern examples. The process goes back at least to the Early Bronze Age and was a useful way of preserving grapes for eating out of season.

Fresh grapes provided a popular and refreshing fruit

Modern white raisins

MASTERS OF WINE
Well-to-do Canaanites of the Late Bronze Age had bronze wine sets made up of a juglet to draw wine from a storage jar, a strainer to filter out any impurities, and a delicate bowl to drink from.

Drinking bowl

Strainer

Juglet

Winemaking

As cities developed in the 3rd millennium B.C., the now large and settled communities of the Holy Land began to grow additional crops. One of the most important was the grape. Vines had probably been brought in from Anatolia sometime during the previous millennium. Now they were widely grown, not only for their fresh fruit, but also for winemaking, and Palestine became renowned for its wines.

SUPPER AT EMMAUS
This painting by Italian artist Caravaggio (1571-1610) reminds us of the importance of mealtimes in early cultures.

ENTER THE CHICKEN

The chicken was domesticated in northern India sometime before 2000 B.C. It was introduced in Egypt by 1400 B.C., but we do not know when it arrived in Palestine. Roast chicken might have been enjoyed by the Israelites, and it was certainly a highly popular food by Roman times.

White cheese, made from cow, goat, or sheep milk, was eaten from at least the Early Bronze Age.

THIRST QUENCHER

The watermelon was widely grown in ancient Egypt and was probably eaten in Palestine from at least the beginning of the Middle Bronze Age (about 2000 B.C.). It was prized as a source of water during dry periods.

Watermelon seeds could be eaten as a food

WHISKED AWAY

This unusual bronze object was found in the "fosse" temple (p. 37) at Lachish. But it was not used in temple rituals. Its similarity to modern Arab utensils shows that it was simply a food whisk.

LATES TO EAT *above*
ircular flaps of unleavened bread
rere made, as they still are today,
y slapping the dough against the
iside wall of a simple cylindrical
ven, called a tannûr. Such bread
aps could be used as edible
latters.

It is not known when cucumbers were introduced into Palestine, but it was probably during the 2nd millennium B.C., by which time they were a common food in Egypt.

OWL FOOD
owling was probably a less important
urce of food than hunting or fishing. But
ese desert partridges, found in the Jordan
lls, especially around the Dead Sea, might
ve provided some variety to the diet.

EGGING THEM ON
he eggs of birds, both domestic and wild, were
valuable foodstuffs. Ostrich eggs, frequently
shown in Egyptian paintings, were especially
ized. The hen's eggs shown here are far smaller
but also nutritious.

*Ancient
Canaanite
vessel*

31

Animals

The scarab beetle was held sacred by the Egyptians; their seals were often made in the shape of scarabs.

Today the Holy Land boasts a rich variety of wildlife, including about 100 species of mammal. Many that were once present have now disappeared. Lions, bears, ostriches, and crocodiles, all mentioned in the Bible, have been hunted to extinction. Archeozoologists are people who study ancient animals, recording and analyzing animal bones found at excavations. Their work can tell us much about the changing relationship between humankind and the animal kingdom. Before the development of agriculture (pp. 26-27), animals were hunted for food and skins. With the advent of stock-rearing, people began to use animals for other products, such as wool and dairy products. The first animals to be domesticated in this way, during the Stone Age, were sheep and goats. In the following Chalcolithic period, pigs and cattle were reared too.

Jesus as the "Good Shepherd" from a 19th-century engraving

TWO BY TWO
Animals were vitally important as a food source, a fact illustrated by the Old Testament story of Noah. He was told by God to bring two of every living thing into the ark to save them from the coming flood.

Hollow snout

POPULAR PLAYTHING *left*
Model animals were popular toys in ancient times, just as they are today. This Iron Age pottery cow from Lachish might have been such a plaything. It could also have been a feeding bottle, since it has a hole in the top and a hollow snout to drink through.

The shy Nubian ibex, or beden, is the "wild goat" the Bible. It is still found in some rocky areas tod.

MONKEY BUSINESS
This amulet shows an ape. Such creatures were imported from Africa in Solomon's reign.

WHAT, A BOAR?
Wild boars, like the one on this amulet from Lachish, can still be found in the thickets that line the Jordan Valley.

SAMSON AND THE LION
In Old Testament times the lion was common in Palestine and often posed a threat to humans and their stock.

BEARS IN THE WOODS
Small, pale-coated Syrian bears lived in Palestine until quite recently. In biblical times they lived in hilly, wooded areas.

SPOTTED IN THE CLIFFS
Leopards were common in Palestine in biblical times – and long after. One was seen in the cliffs at En Gedi as recently as 1974.

PAYMENT TO THE KING
The Black Obelisk is a monument put up in Nimrud to commemorate 31 military campaigns of the Assyrian king Shalmaneser III. This detail from the obelisk shows some of the tribute paid to the king by the ruler of Sukha in Syria. It depicts two lions and a deer, animals native to the middle Euphrates area. The artist could not have seen many lions, since he has given them jackal tails!

LUCKY DUCK
The duck was a popular source of food and was often a subject for artists. This ivory duck from Lachish was probably the decorative end of a cosmetic spoon.

IN THE STABLE
The importance of meat- and milk-producing animals is shown by the presence of such creatures in engravings like this Nativity by Gustave Doré (1832-83).

THREE WISE MEN
The wise men ride one-humped Arabian camels, which were domesticated in Egypt before 3000 B.C. and were familiar in Palestine by 1500 B.C. Two-humped Bactrian camels appeared during the Iron Age.

Clothing

BECAUSE ITEMS like textiles are only occasionally preserved, archeologists have to rely on paintings, sculptures, and models for their evidence of what people wore in the earliest times. The earliest people probably clothed themselves in animal skins. But spinning and weaving date back to at least the 7th millennium B.C., as shown by a remarkable discovery of preserved organic material (made from plants or animals) at Nahal Hemar in the Judean Desert. Some equipment for making cloth also survives, to give us further clues. Later people wore clothes made of a variety of materials often brightly colored with natural dyes. Leather and felt were also used, for shoes and hats as well as clothes.

EGYPTIAN INFLUENCE
The well-traveled Phoenicians had great knowledge of the costumes of many countries. A Phoenician carved this ivory panel showing a figure wearing royal Egyptian-style garments.

HIGH AND MIGHTY
Clothing could show social status. This rich woman of the 10th century B.C. wears an elaborate headdress.

TOOLS FOR THE LOOM
It is not always clear how these bone weaving tools were used. The spatula was probably slipped between the vertical warp threads on the loom and forced upward to close up the horizontal weft threads.

OFF-THE-SHOULDER
These Israelites wear skullcaps, long kilts, and cloaks draped over one shoulder, leaving the other shoulder exposed. The kilts and cloaks are shown fringed and were probably woven in brightly colored patterns.

LOOM WEIGHT *below*
Often made of unbaked clay, these were used to weigh down the vertical warp threads of the loom.

Spatula

Point, or awl

REBEKAH
This is a painting of Rebekah, wife of Isaac in the Book of Genesis, at the well. It illustrates the 19th-century idea of costume in Old Testament times.

IN A SPIN *above*
In the process of spinning, fibers are twisted together to make a continuous thread. To do this people used a stick with a type of "flywheel" on it to give it momentum. These objects are called "spindle whorls" and are often found on excavations in the Holy Land.

SAFETY PIN
After about 1000 B.C. toggle pins began to be replaced as garment fasteners by "fibulae," which were like safety pins. This one belongs to the Persian period.

Eye

BUTTONED UP
Toggle pins of bronze or gold were used to fasten garments. The pin was attached by means of its "eye" to one side; a string was sewn on the other side. To fasten the garment, the string was wound around the pin, like the toggle on a duffle coat.

Middle Bronze Age toggle pins

Pattern of original textile

HEADGEAR
The Canaanites were very fond of head and hair ornaments. This delicate golden headband from Tell el-'Ajjul dates to the 16th century B.C.

UNDER THE VEIL
These women and children are being taken prisoner after the capture of Lachish (p. 46). The scene shows typical Judean women's costume – a long, loose tunic and a veil covering the hair which extends the entire length of the tunic.

TRACES OF TEXTILE
Many of the 12th-century B.C. graves at Tell es-Sa'idiyeh, Jordan, contain bronze objects wrapped in cloth. In such cases the corrosion of the metal has preserved the textile. This javelin has been wrapped in fine Egyptian linen.

SANDALS
Made with a piece of leather cut to the shape of the foot and tied with thongs or cords, such sandals were widely worn in the Holy Land from at least 2000 B.C. This well-preserved example dates to the Roman period and was found at Masada (p. 55).

Very fine, flexible metal allowed band to be wrapped around head

Roman sandal designs

Gold earrings of the Roman period from Lachish

Jewelry

THE NEED TO ADORN the body using jewelry and cosmetics must have been felt from the very earliest times. Such decorations could be used to show the wearer's social status or wealth, or to express religious beliefs. Simple beads and pendants of bone, shell, and stone are often found in prehistoric graves. The value placed on such items is clear from the amount of skill and time that went into their manufacture. These materials were used long after the techniques of gold and silver working had been learned. In the hands of the Canaanite craftsmen of the Middle and Late Bronze Ages, jewelry became a highly accomplished art form. The goldwork displays sophisticated techniques such as repoussé (raising the surface in relief by hammering from behind) and granulation (the use of tiny grains of metal). The Israelites did not learn these skills, but they were inherited by the Phoenicians, whose jewelry was widely sought after.

SILVER GRAINS
This Iron Age silver earring has fine granulated decoration.

HOLLOW GOLD
This gold earring from the Persian period is made up of hollow spheres.

HAIR DRESSING
The finest hair combs were made of bone or ivory and were often ornamented with finely carved geometric or naturalistic designs.

FOR FACE PAINTING
During the Early Bronze Age, hollowed-out and finely engraved animal bones were used as containers for cosmetics such as eye makeup.

PENDANTS
These unusual bone pendants from Lachish, dating to the Iron Age, probably had some significance in addition to being decorative. The varying numbers of dot and circle motifs suggest that some might have served as calendars or reckoners. Another suggestion is that a group of such pendants would be unstrung and thrown on the ground, and the resulting pattern used for looking into the future.

Lengths of beaten bronze could be easily bent to the right size

Bangles and anklets were a popular form of jewelry in the Iron Age.

Faience bead

THREADING THEM THROUGH *above*
Like most Canaanite necklaces, this one was found without its original thread. The arrangement of the beads is therefore quite arbitrary.

BEAUTIFUL BLUES *above*
During the Late Bronze Age, many beads were made of faience, a blue glazed material consisting mainly of quartz.

HOLY OFFERING
In the "fosse" temple, a Late Bronze Age Canaanite sanctuary at Lachish, a number of gold pendants were found. They probably formed part of an offering to the deity.

Decoration formed by impression made when gold is beaten over a patterned object

TOUCH OF GLAMOR
Jewelry worn by actress Vivien Leigh in her role as Cleopatra was based on Middle Eastern originals. Notice the headband and jeweled earrings.

Traces of linen

EGYPTIAN PLANTS
Many Late Bronze Age beads and pendants show strong Egyptian influence. The palmettes on this necklace are a typical motif.

Palmette

BELOW THE BELT
The lower part of an Iron Age terra-cotta figure clearly shows two pairs of anklets of the type shown opposite.

FISH OUT OF WATER
Toward the end of the Late Bronze Age, many objects made in Egypt were imported into Canaan. This fine ivory cosmetic box in the shape of a fish was found inside the bronze bowl in an unusual 12th-century B.C. grave at Tell es-Sa'idiyeh. The bowl had been strapped over the genitals of the deceased using Egyptian linen, traces of which still remain.

Money and trade

T HE HOLY LAND is at the heart of the Fertile Crescent (p. 29). This made it a corridor for international traders. Merchants traveled between Egypt and Arabia in the south, Anatolia and Mesopotamia in the north; there was also maritime (sea) trade with the Mediterranean islands. These contacts go back a long way. In the New Stone Age period there was trade in obsidian, a black volcanic glass that was used to make tools. But it was the growth of cities in the third millennium B.C. that really laid the foundations for the trade that would sustain the civilizations of the area for thousands of years. In Palestine, farming developed so that surpluses of cereals, flour, oil, and wine could be exported to foreign markets. Canaanite arts and craft objects were also exported widely. Raw materials such as wood and metal came in from abroad.

Found at Amathus in Cyprus, this Phoenician glass vessel was probably used to hold incense

WEIGHING THEM UP
Before coins were invented, commercial deals were done using a variety of materials. Metal ingots or scraps were often used as a currency of established value, and they had to be weighed so that their worth could be assessed. So accurate weights were needed, like these lion-shaped ones from Assyria. They are inscribed with the name of King Shalmaneser III, for whom they were made.

During their first revolt against Rome in A.D. 66 (p. 55), the Jews struck their own coins

WAGON TRAIN
A pottery model of a covered wagon from Hamman in Syria shows the type of vehicle that was used to transport goods in the late 3rd millennium B.C. Wagons like this might have been used by traveling metalworkers, peddling their wares from town to town.

SHEKEL
The standard Jewish silver coin was the shekel, which was also a unit of weight. This coin, from the first Jewish revolt, is inscribed "Jerusalem the holy."

STOPPING ON THE WAY
This detail of an evocative painting by Edward Lear (1812-1888) shows a desert caravan stopping by Mount Sinai. It gives a good idea of what long-distance caravan traffic must have been like in ancient times.

ROMAN CASH
Coins came into common use in the Holy Land at the time of the conquest of Alexander (p. 54). Roman imperial coins bore a portrait of the emperor, in this case, Vespasian.

A coin of the second Jewish revolt (A.D. 132-135) bears the name of its leader, Simon Bar Kochba

ONE HUMP OR TWO?
Two-humped Bactrian camels appear on the Assyrian Black Obelisk (p. 33). These creatures did not appear in the Holy Land until Solomon's time. Before that, trading caravans relied on the one-humped Arabian camel.

MAN OF THE PEOPLE?
These bronze coins are from the reign of Herod's son Archelaus (4 B.C.–A.D. 6). One shows a crested helmet, the other a bunch of grapes. The Greek inscription reads "Herod, governor of the people."

Because coins circulated widely, they could be used to promote a cause or idea. These two from the second Jewish revolt bear inscriptions. The first reads "Year one of the redemption of Israel"; the second bears the name of the leader Simon Bar Kochba.

POPPY POWER
During the Late Bronze Age little jugs known as "bil-bils" were imported into Canaan. Analysis of substances found inside some of them has shown that they were used to hold the drug opium. The shape of the jug is strikingly like that of an upturned poppy head.

Continued on next page

A bronze coin of Agrippa I (A.D. 37-44), grandson of Herod the Great. He used the umbrella as a symbol of monarchy.

INSTEAD OF MONEY
Precious metals were frequently traded as ingots. This silver ingot is from Zinjirli, ancient Sam'al.

TURNING THE TABLES
Jesus of Nazareth objected to merchants trading their wares in the precincts of the Temple in Jerusalem and toppled the stalls and tables.

COMMEMORATION
Coins could be made to commemorate famous events. This coin, inscribed "Judaea Capta," records the Roman victory in the first Jewish revolt (p. 55).

Handles of this shape give this vessel the name "stirrup jar"

IMPORT
Beautifully made and elegantly decorated, Mycenaean vessels known as "stirrup jars" were imported into Canaan during the Late Bronze Age, perhaps containing perfumed oils.

MERCHANT SHIP OF SOLOMON'S FLEET
King Solomon was intent upon developing a wide network of sea trade relations. With the co-operation of Hiram, king of Tyre, he built a major port at Ezion Geber at the head of the Red Sea. A joint Israelite and Phoenician fleet was based there, and every three years, ships set sail for "Ophir" (probably the Somali coast of East Africa) in search of fine gold.

STORAGE JAR
In the 12th century B.C., Tell es-Sa'idiyeh, on the eastern side of the Jordan River, was an Egyptian taxation and distribution center, collecting produce from Jordan for shipment to Egypt. Jars of Egyptian design were found in one of the storerooms at the site and may have been used to store and transport wine.

SEA HORSES
Timber was always a valuable item of trade. The most expensive and sought-after wood came from the "Cedars of Lebanon." This 8th-century B.C. Assyrian relief shows Phoenician merchant ships hauling logs along the Syrian coast. These ships were called hippoi, meaning horses, as they had horse figureheads.

8 shekels

"Neseph," five sixths of a shekel

"Beqa," half a shekel

HOW HEAVY?
The ancient Palestinian system of weights was based on the shekel (equivalent to about 0.4 oz [11.4 g]), the mina (60 shekels) and the kikkar or "talent" (60 minas). These stone weights are inscribed in Hebrew with their value.

LONG-DISTANCE TRADER *above*
This Roman merchant ship, known as a corbita, has two masts. Its sails are made of oblong blocks of cloth sewn together and reinforced with leather patches at the corners. Such vessels were used for long-distance shipping across the Mediterranean rather than for coastal use.

LIGHTING THE WAY
Pharos, the lighthouse of Alexandria, the port city and capital of Egypt founded by Alexander the Great, was one of the seven wonders of the ancient world.

ROYAL PURPLE
One of the most sought-after items traded by Phoenician merchants was their purple-dyed cloth. By the time of the Roman Empire, its prestige was so great that it could only be worn by the emperor.

THEIR TRUE COLORS
The highly prized purple dye for which the Phoenicians are renowned was extracted from a gland of the murex snail. Each snail yielded only a drop of yellow liquid which darkened on exposure to light. Processing required slow simmering for about two weeks. Up to 60,000 snails were needed for each pound of dye. Different tints were achieved by varying the amount of extract from different species.

Arts and crafts

SOME OF THE EARLIEST PEOPLE of the Holy Land were skilled in the arts and crafts, producing items of beauty for religious purposes and as status symbols. Those who made the lime-plaster statues found at 'Ain Ghazal (pp. 8-9) in the Stone Age had great expertise. They also displayed great refinement in the way they applied the decoration to the statues. Wonderfully carved ivories and elaborate copper objects are found in the following Chalcolithic period. But it was the Canaanites of the Bronze Age and the Phoenicians of the Iron Age who turned this tradition of skillful work into a real industry, producing arts and crafts that were much admired and sought after throughout the eastern Mediterranean and beyond.

FOR SHOW
In the Middle Bronze Age, metal-casting techniques became more and more sophisticated. This bronze axhead, decorated with a lion fighting a dog, was probably for ceremonial use.

Incised alphabetic writing

MUSIC MAKERS
Dancing and music were undoubtedly popular activities throughout the history of Palestine, although few instruments have survived. Written descriptions and pictures suggest the use of a wide variety of instruments, such as harps, lyres, flutes, trumpets, and a range of percussion instruments.

WRITING IT DOWN
The art of writing using alphabetic letters was begun by the Canaanites (pp. 16-17). One of the earliest attempts at alphabetic script was found on this 17th-century B.C. bronze dagger from Lachish.

DAILY LIFE IN ANCIENT JERICHO
Wooden furniture was preserved in some of the tombs in Jericho. Canaanite carpenters had an extensive tool kit. They put their products together using accurate joints and deco-rated them with carving.

IVORY QUEENS
The Canaanites and Phoenicians were renowned for their ivory carving. Ivory was often used for inlays and furniture ornaments. Some ivory objects have letters on the back to show where they should be attached. This example is a 9th-century Phoenician ivory from the Assyrian city of Nimrud. It shows two seated queens in Egyptian style and was decorated with blue glass and gold overlay.

HARD TO CARVE

The combat between a lion and a dog seems to have been a popular subject for the Canaanites. This example is carved on a piece of black basalt, a very hard stone which took great skill to work. It dates to the 14th century B.C. and comes from Beth Shan.

Applied gold decoration

Most of the methods of the ancient potter are still used today. Here a village potter in Egypt produces simple domestic wares.

SYRIAN STYLE

This ivory female head was found at Nimrud. Its style of carving lacks the sophistication of the Phoenician piece opposite. It might have been the work of a Syrian carver.

Granulation

FUNNY FACE

The finest pottery ever seen in Palestine, in terms of both technical quality and beauty, was made by the Canaanites. Their potters also had a sense of humor, as shown by this extraordinary face vase from Jericho, dating to the 6th century B.C.

GOLDEN GRAINS

This fine pendant comes from Tell el-'Ajjul and dates to the 16th century B.C. It is decorated by granulation. In this process gold wire is melted to make tiny beads, which are then soldered to the surface.

CARVED IN STONE

Vessels carved from stone such as calcite and alabaster were extremely popular in the Late Bronze and Iron Ages, perhaps as containers for perfumed oil. This example comes from Tell es-Sa'idiyeh.

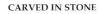

TREASURES OF THE TEMPLE

When the Egyptians left Canaan they took the best artists and craftworkers. So Solomon asked the king of Tyre for Phoenician artisans when building his temple in Jerusalem. Phoenician metalworkers probably made the temple furnishings mentioned in the Bible and shown in this old engraving.

War and weapons

From the earliest times weapons were used for hunting and to protect people against their enemies. Until copper smelting was invented sometime before 4000 B.C., the people of the Holy Land made weapons out of wood, bone, and stone. As the Early Bronze Age cities grew, the techniques of warfare developed and armies were established. The more advanced metalworking of this period provided soldiers with mass-produced swords, spears, and axes. Initially these were made of copper, later of bronze. Later in the Bronze Age war and weapons became more sophisticated, with field battles involving cavalry and chariots; well-defended cities were attacked using special siege equipment. The Philistines probably brought ironworking to Canaan around 1200 B.C; after this, iron weapons gradually replaced bronze ones.

This relief shows an Aramean cavalryman of the 9th century B.C. It comes from Tell Halaf, the biblical Gozan.

Pair of helmets from the Persian period

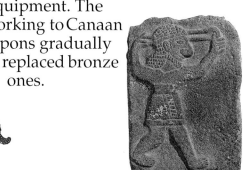

GIANT-SLAYER
One of the most ancient of all weapons was the sling. Because slings were made of leather or cloth, few examples have survived, but groups of slingshots (either shaped "bullets" of clay or smooth, rounded pebbles) are frequently found. The Bible recounts how David killed the Philistine leader Goliath using a sling – a most plausible story given the deadly accuracy of this powerful weapon.

TAKING AIM
This slinger is depicted on a 9th-century B.C. relief from the royal palace at Tell Halaf (Gozan), Syria.

GOOD GRIP
The hilt of this Late Bronze Age dagger from Alalakh in Syria was cast with deep recesses to allow a wooden or bone grip to be inserted.

Broad cutting blade

Ridge to make blade stronger

Sword would have been attached to wooden or bone hilt with copper rivets

Axe

Sickle sword

Shield

This archer has a composite bow, a powerful weapon made of layers of wood, glue, horn, and sinew.

SOCKETED SPEAR
During the Middle Bronze Age, improved casting techniques made it possible to make spear and javelin heads with a hollow socket to take a shaft.

Socket

AX-MAN
This bronze warrior figure of the Middle Bronze Age holds a distinctive ax with a head shaped like a duck's bill. The figure with its "duckbill" ax was found in the early part of this period (about 1800 B.C.).

LEGIONARY
During the Roman period, a highly organized army helped the emperors keep control of their vast territories. This soldier holds the standard of his legion.

ARMED TO THE TEETH
This Middle Bronze Age warrior holds a spear and a "sickle sword," a type of weapon now known from several examples found on sites in both Canaan and Egypt. A sickle sword is shown being carried by one of the Canaanites on the Egyptian Beni Hasan wall paintings (pp. 10-11).

Tang for attaching to shaft

KEEPING IT ALL TOGETHER
Early Bronze Age copper javelins with long "tangs" were tightly lashed to their wooden shafts with leather thongs.

HORSEPOWER
The Canaanites used two-horse chariots as light and fast fighting vehicles. This later Greek chariot was drawn by four horses.

Thin blade, suitable for stabbing

HEAVYWEIGHT WEAPON
During the final phase of the Early Bronze Age (the time of the patriarchs, pp. 10-11), city life in Canaan declined, and the people moved into the country-side. Metal weapons became larger and heavier, more suited to the harsher conditions this change in lifestyle entailed. This sword from Beit Dagin, near Tel Aviv, Israel, is one of the largest known weapons of this period.

45

Continued on next page

The siege of Lachish

The northern kingdom of Israel came to an end in 722 B.C. with the capture of its capital, Samaria, by the Assyrians. The southern kingdom of Judah was also forced to submit to the might of the Assyrians, and although Hezekiah (715-686 B.C.) rebelled against the Assyrian king Sennacherib in 704 B.C., the attempt was a disaster. In 701 B.C. Sennacherib swept into Judah and destroyed many cities, including Lachish. The siege and capture of this city are vividly depicted in a series of limestone reliefs from Sennacherib's palace at Nineveh. The Assyrians finally advanced on Jerusalem, where Hezekiah was forced to submit and pay heavy tribute.

Flaming torches thrown down by the defenders

Broken ladder – used by the Assyrians for scaling but pushed down by the defenders

Battering ram – the soldier at the front is pouring water over the front of the machine so that it won't catch fire

MIGHTY MAN
This painting by 19th-century artist William Dyce shows Joash, son of Shemaah of Gibeah, who was one of David's heroes.

ARROWHEADS
When bronze became freely available after 2000 B.C., arrowheads made of the metal were used widely. Iron arrowheads came in after about 1100 B.C.

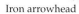

Selection of bronze arrowheads

Iron arrowhead

DOWN WITH THE WALLS
The battering ram may have been developed as early as the Middle Bronze Age. It continued to provide an effective way of attacking defensive walls until the development of explosives.

TORTOISE SHELL
The Romans used stout swords and big rectangular shields. In close formations, especially when attacking cities, soldiers would lock their shields together to form a solid wall or roof. This formation was known as a *testudo,* or tortoise.

BETTER BATTLE-AXES
During the period of the patriarchs, toward the end of the third millennium B.C., battle-axes were developed that could be secured to the handle by means of a socket. They were highly effective in piercing metal helmets – and cracking skulls!

Ax head with handle

DUCK'S BILL
During the Middle Bronze Age, ax blades were made longer to produce the so-called "duckbill" ax.

Parapet of round shields on top of city gatehouse

Judean archers and slingers defending the gatehouse

Large hooded shield

Assyrian archer – the pointed helmet was effective protection against vertically falling showers of arrows

Assyrian spearman with crested helmet

Siege ramps of banked-up earth covered with logs

Deportees leaving the gate, bound for exile in Assyria, carrying with them a few possessions in bags

Bronze scale armor like this was worn by the Assyrians during the siege of Lachish

A 19th-century impression of scale armor

This Roman catapult could hurl rocks over long distances. It was called an *onager* (wild ass) because of its kicking action.

The Assyrians

HEROIC STRUGGLE
In spite of their warlike image, the Assyrians greatly appreciated art and fine craftsmanship. This carved ivory plaque shows a hero or king fighting a lion. It was made locally in Assyria.

THE KINGDOM OF ASSYRIA was centered on the valley of the Tigris River in northern Iraq. It had existed since at least 2000 B.C. During the 9th century B.C., the Assyrian kings began to expand their territory, both to secure their boundaries and to gain control of trade routes. The next 200 years saw the relentless advance of the Assyrian armies in regular campaigns against Syria, Phoenicia, and ultimately Israel and Judah. The kings of these states could buy a little time by paying tribute to the Assyrians – taxes in the form of treasures or other goods – but failure to meet the increasing demands, or any form of resistance, was met by crushing retaliation. Territories conquered by the Assyrians were added to the growing empire. In 722 B.C. the northern kingdom of Israel effectively came to an end with the taking of its capital, Samaria, and the loss of part of its population through the Assyrian policy of moving people from their homelands. Judah survived longer, but only by paying crippling tribute. Many of the exploits of the Assyrians are shown on carved stone slabs made to adorn the royal palaces.

HOUSEHOLD GOD
The Assyrians often place figures of gods beneath th floors of their houses and palaces to keep out evil demons. This one is the go Lahmu, "the hairy."

THE EMPIRE'S SPREAD
At its greatest extent, in the early 7th century B.C., the Assyrian Empire covered a vast area, stretching from Iran to Egypt.

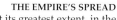
Bottle

FOR HOME AND PALACE
These two vessels show the skill and artistry of the Assyrian potter. The elegant, thin-walled beaker on the left is an example of "Assyrian palace ware." On the right is a small bottle, beautifully decorated in multicolored glaze. Both pieces date to the 8th-7th centuries B.C.

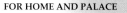
Beaker

WAR GODDESS
This bronze plaque shows Ishtar, the most important goddess of the Assyrians. Here she is depicted as the goddess of war, carrying arms and mounted on her favorite animal, the lion. Ishtar was the equivalent of the Canaanite goddess Astarte (pp. 24-25).

TRIBUTE FROM PHOENICIA
Carved ivories were often used to decorate furniture. This panel from the Assyrian capital, Nimrud, showing a woman wearing an Egyptian-style wig, was made by a Phoenician craftworker. It was probably brought back in the 8th century B.C. from one of the western campaigns as part of war booty or tribute.

GODDESS OF LOVE
This blue plaque showing a winged goddess comes from the temple of Ninurta at Nimrud. It dates to the 9th century B.C. The goddess is probably Ishtar, shown in her guise as goddess of love.

Blue color typical of Assyrian decorative wares

LION'S SHARE
Lions were a popular subject in Assyrian art. This one might originally have been attached to the handle of a fan.

PAYMENTS TO THE KING
The military campaigns of the Assyrian king Shalmaneser III (858-824 B.C.) were commemorated on a stone monument, now known as the Black Obelisk, which was set up in the capital, Nimrud. One of the scenes shows Jehu, king of Israel, giving tribute to Shalmaneser. The kneeling figure may not be Jehu himself, but a representative. The tribute itself is shown on another panel.

MAKING YOUR MARK
Small stone cylinders with a hole through them were carved with a design and rolled out on clay tablets or jar or parcel sealings. The resulting impression acted as a signature or mark of ownership. This chalcedony seal, dating to around 750 B.C., shows a heroic figure grasping two ostriches by the neck.

STATEROOM
The richly decorated throne room of King Ashurnasirpal II at Nimrud is shown here reconstructed by a 19th-century artist. The carved reliefs, which today are seen as plain stone, were originally brightly painted.

The Babylonians

MESOPOTAMIA, THE LAND BETWEEN the Tigris and Euphrates rivers in what is now Iraq, was one of the earliest centers of civilization in the Middle East. At the start of the 2nd millennium B.C., the Amorites, a people originally from the Syrian desert, founded a dynasty at the city of Babylon on the Euphrates. In the 18th century B.C., under King Hammurabi, the Babylonians achieved supremacy over the whole of Mesopotamia, establishing an empire that stretched from Mari in the northwest to Elam in the east. This "Old Babylonian" period was brought to an end by the Hittite King Mursilis I, who attacked Babylonia in 1595 B.C. and destroyed the city of Babylon. In the 7th century B.C., the city's fortunes improved when the local official Nabopolassar took control of southern Mesopotamia and assumed kingship of Babylon, founding the Neo-Babylonian dynasty.

Stone maceheads were often dedicated to the gods and placed in temples. This one is dedicated to Nergal, god of disease.

BUILDER
Bronze figures showing a king carrying a basket filled with building materials were placed in the foundations of temples. The inscription gives the names of the king and the god of the temple.

NABOPOLASSAR'S EMPIRE
In 612 B.C., Nabopolassar overthrew the Assyrians and laid claim to their lands, including Judah. His son Nebuchadnezzar raided Judah in 597 B.C. after a rebellion. When revolt broke out again ten years later, Nebuchadnezzar responded with a devastating campaign which destroyed Jerusalem.

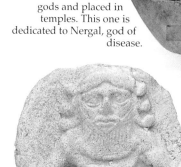

AGE OF AQUARIUS
The Babylonians are thought to have invented the zodiac. This terra-cotta plaque shows a giant carrying streams of water – the ancestor of Aquarius.

GREAT GATE
Nebuchadnezzar rebuilt Babylon. One of the most impressive buildings was the Ishtar Gate, which gave access to the processional road leading to the main temple.

TOWER OR TEMPLE? *right*
According to the book of Genesis, the Tower of Babel was built by the descendants of Noah in order to reach Heaven. This is a reference to Babylon's ziggurat or temple tower. This depiction of the tower is from a detail of a painting by Pieter Bruegel the elder (1525-69).

N THE BOUNDARY

 the Old Babylonian period, allocations of
 nd and tax concessions granted to
 dividuals or districts were recorded on
 ay tablets. A more public way of
 cording such agreements was the
 oundary stone, an elaborately
 rved and inscribed stone set
 p in the temple or the field
 which the agreement
 lated. The symbols on
 e stone represent the
 ods and goddesses
 ho witnessed the
 ntract.

 he planet Venus,
 presenting Ishtar,
 oddess of love and
 rtility

Snake symbol of the
underworld god Ishtaran

Moon, representing the
moon god Sin

Sun, representing the
sun god Shamash

Nabu, god of writing,
seen here as a wedge-
shaped (cuneiform)
symbol

Scorpion,
symbol of
the goddess
Ishhara

Altars
and
shrines

The Persians

Wealthy or important people sewed ornaments like this onto their clothes.

ORIGINALLY FROM CENTRAL ASIA, the Persians moved into western Iran during the second millennium B.C. and settled in Parsa (now Fars). Their early history is closely linked to that of the Medes, who settled in the same region. In alliance with the Babylonians, the Medes, under their king Cyaxares, overthrew the Assyrian state in 612 B.C. In 550 B.C. Cyrus of the house of Achaemenes deposed his grandfather, the Median king Astyages, and became undisputed ruler of both Medes and Persians. The Achaemenid Empire was born, and began to increase its power. Soon Cyrus had added much of western Anatolia to his territories. In 539 B.C. he defeated Babylonia and inherited its empire, which included Syria and Palestine. It was during the reign of Cyrus that the Jews were allowed to return to Palestine. The rebuilding of Jerusalem and its temple are described in the Books of Ezra and Nehemiah.

THE ACHAEMENID EMPIRE
At its maximum extent during the reign of Darius I (522-486 B.C.), the empire stretched from Egypt and Libya in the west to the Indus River in the east.

GLAMOROUS GOAT
This silver goat is said to come from Persepolis and dates to the 5th century B.C.

ON GUARD
This Persian palace guard is portrayed on a glazed brick frieze from Susa.

ROYAL CENTER
Persepolis was an important civic and religious center built by Darius I and his successor Xerxes (486-465 B.C.). It is shown here in an imaginative 19th-century reconstruction.

Cuneiform (wedge-shaped) script

LION AT BAY
A royal lion hunt is portrayed on this impression of an agate cylinder seal. The inscription records the name "Darius the Great King," probably Darius I.

Ahuramazda, the supreme god of the Persians

FINERY FROM AFAR
The Persian kings employed artists and craftworkers of many nationalities, and foreign influence can be seen in many of their works of art. The applied golden figures on this silver bowl show a winged lion with the head of the Egyptian dwarf god Bes, wearing a feathered crown.

Spout to take wick

LIGHT ON THE SUBJECT
Dating to the 6th century B.C., this bronze lamp was found in the "Solar shrine" at Lachish, a small temple associated with sun worship.

HIGH CEREMONY
This imaginative reconstruction shows one of the ceremonies that might have taken place at Persepolis.

CYRUS CYLINDER
The text on this clay cylinder tells how Cyrus allowed people in captivity in Babylon to return to their homelands. It does not mention the Jews, but it was this policy that allowed them to return to Palestine.

The Greeks and Romans

THE VAST EMPIRE of the Persians was taken over by the Macedonian ruler Alexander the Great in 332 B.C. When Alexander died nine years later, Palestine first came under the control of his general Ptolemy and Ptolemy's descendants, then passed to the rule of the Seleucids, a dynasty based in Syria. In 167 B.C., the Seleucid king Antiochus IV sacked and looted the Temple in Jerusalem and forbade Jewish religious practices. The Jews revolted and, through a series of brilliant military campaigns, were able to defeat the Seleucids and secure a brief period of independence for Judah (about 142-63 B.C.). This period, of the so-called Hasmonean kingdom, was brought to an end by a bitter civil war which was only stopped when Rome, the power that finally drove the Seleucids from Syria, intervened. In 63 B.C. the Roman general Pompey entered Jerusalem. The area, now called Judea, was given semi-independence in 40 B.C., when the Roman senate, in recognition of his loyalty to Rome, appointed Herod king. Herod's son Archelaus succeeded his father in 4 B.C., but he was unsatisfactory as a ruler. In A.D. 6 he was dismissed by the Roman emperor Augustus, leaving Judea as a Roman province, ruled by officials called procurators.

TIME OF CHANGE
Alexander the Great had a vast empire stretching from Greece to western India. The period when Palestine was part of this empire was one of change for the area. Longstanding traditions were overturned in the process of "Hellenism," the full-scale importing of Greek (and later, Roman) culture, including art, architecture, religion, and language.

WHERE THE ROMAN WRIT RAN
By the time of the Roman emperor Titus, the entire Mediterranean area was under Roman rule.

FROM GREECE TO EGYPT
When Alexander died, his empire was fought over by his generals. Ptolemy I, a Macedonian, seized Egypt and Palestine, and founded a dynasty that ruled from a new capital, Alexandria, in Egypt. The Ptolemies were Greek but were often portrayed as traditional Egyptian rulers. This painted limestone stela shows Ptolemy II, who succeeded his father in 283 B.C.

PORTABLE ALTAR
This miniature bronze altar of the Roman period comes from Byblos. Once an important Phoenician city and port, Byblos became a minor town in the Roman period.

SACRIFICE TO THE GODS
The enforced worship of pagan Greek and Roman gods and goddesses was deeply resented by the Jews.

JEWISH REVOLTS

In A.D. 66 a Jewish revolt against Roman rule, led by priests and members of the sect of Pharisees, broke out in Palestine. The revolt was put down with great severity by the emperor Vespasian, together with his son Titus, who, in A.D. 70, captured Jerusalem and destroyed the Temple. The last stronghold of the Jews was Masada, which fell to the Romans in A.D. 74 after the mass suicide of the defenders. A second revolt in A.D. 132 was crushed by the emperor Hadrian.

Marble bust of the Roman emperor Tiberius

ARCH OF TITUS

The Roman victory in the first Jewish war was commemorated in sculpted friezes on a magnificent arch in Rome. The arch was erected by the emperor Domitian in memory of his brother Titus.

CRUCIFIXION

This reconstruction shows how Jesus might have been crucified.

This amusing Roman "face" juglet from Jerusalem was made in a mold. It dates to the 2nd century A.D.

CALVARY

After A.D. 6 Judea was a province of the Roman Empire, run by procurators. It was under the fifth procurator, Pontius Pilate (A.D. 27-30), that Jesus Christ was crucified.

NEW GODS FOR OLD

The Greeks and Romans introduced their own gods and goddesses. In Phoenicia, where Canaanite religion had persisted until the coming of Alexander, most of the new gods could be related to the old gods. The "new" goddess Aphrodite, shown here in a bronze statue from Byblos, was identified with the Canaanite and Phoenician fertility goddess Astarte (pp. 24-25).

ROMAN BURIALS

During the Roman period burial was a two-stage process. After death, the body was wrapped in linen, sprinkled with perfume, and placed on a shelf inside a tomb. After some time, when the flesh had decayed, the relatives would enter the tomb, gather up the bones, and place them in a stone box called an ossuary.

King Herod

HEROD WAS THE SON OF ANTIPATER, adviser to John Hyrcanus, the last of the Hasmonean rulers. When the Roman general Pompey entered Jerusalem in 63 B.C. and outraged the Jewish community by entering the Holy of Holies (p. 21), Hyrcanus and Antipater were shrewd enough to avoid conflict. They skillfully walked a political tightrope during the power struggle between Julius Caesar and Pompey, changing allegiance to Caesar at just the right time. Herod was clever too, at first backing Mark Antony, then changing to support Antony's victorious rival, Augustus. In this way Herod was seen as a friend o Rome and was rewarded by being made king of Judea in 40 B.C.

HEROD'S WORLD
At its maximum extent Herod's kingdom took in most of Palestine, parts of southern Syria, and large areas east of the Jordan River.

Round eastern tower

Encircling corridor on several levels

Underground passage and marble steps leading from base of hill to vaulted entrance chamber

Eastern half of palace area occupied by garden enclosed by columns

Tyre

Tiberias

Jerusalem
Herodium

Masada

WILD WOMAN
John the Baptist, whose head was brought to Salome, was a prisoner at Herod's fortress at Machaerus. The story is shown in a detail of a painting by Lucas Cranach (1472-1553).

WELL APPOINTED
The western half of the palace area at Herodium contained living quarters and service rooms. On the north side was this impressive bathhouse. It was richly ornamented with mosaic floors and frescoes (paintings on plaster).

HERODIUM *right and below*
Herod was a great builder. Little has survived of his greatest achievement, the rebuilt Temple at Jerusalem. But excavations of his palatial mountaintop fortress around the Jordan Valley and the Dead Sea have shown something of the splendor of his architecture. Herod's hilltop fortress of Herodium, 7 miles (12 km) south of Jerusalem, is a good example. It contained a luxurious palace and was also Herod's burial place. The picture shows an aerial view of the site today; the model is a reconstruction of what it looked like in Herod's time.

WALL OF TEARS
The Wailing Wall at Jerusalem is part of the western retaining wall of the huge sanctuary that contained Herod's Temple at its center.

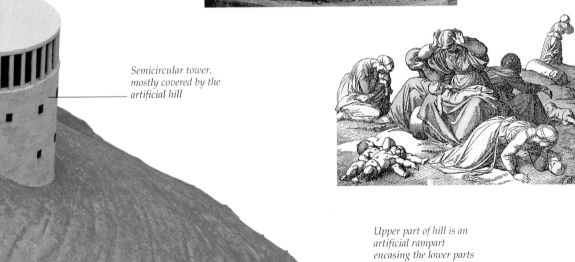

Semicircular tower, mostly covered by the artificial hill

Upper part of hill is an artificial rampart encasing the lower parts of the fortress

MASSACRE OF THE INNOCENTS
According to the New Testament, it was Herod the Great (Herod I) who was responsible for the slaughter of the children in his attempt to dispose of Jesus of Nazareth. In reality the story is a myth.

MASADA
At Masada, later to become famous during the first Jewish revolt, Herod added to the existing buildings a series of huge water cisterns, storehouses for ammunition and food, and a luxurious palace constructed on three natural rock terraces.

The Bible as evidence

THE BIBLE AS WE KNOW IT today is not a single book, but a collection of 63 individual books divided into two main parts, the Old and New Testaments. For archeologists working in the Holy Land, the Bible is a major source, containing a wealth of historical, religious, philosophical, socio-logical, literary, and poetic material. But it must, like any other ancient collection of texts, be used critically. Many of the Old Testament books are edited compi-lations, put into their final form a long time after the events they describe. The development of the Bible and the disentangling of the various strands that form its books are fields of study in their own right.

DEAD SEA SCROLLS
In 1947 a goatherd stumbled into a cave at Qumran, Jordan. It contained the ancient Hebrew manuscripts now called the Dead Sea Scrolls. They had been stored in jars like this one. Although incomplete and fragmentary, the scrolls must originally have included all of the books of the Old Testament and Apocrypha. They are the oldest versions of the texts known so far.

One of the Dead Sea Scrolls contains the text of the Book of the prophet Habakkuk, together with a commentary in which the words of the prophet are set against con-temporary events

THE BIBLE IN GREEK
The 4th-century A.D. Codex Sinaiticus is inscribed in Greek capital letters in ink on parchment. It was discovered at St. Catherine's monastery, right.

HIDING PLACE OF THE SCROLLS
Caves in the Judean Desert, close to the Dead Sea, were the hiding places of the Scrolls. They probably came from the library of Qumran, the monastery of the Essenes, a highly religious group of Jews. The scrolls were put in the caves to protect them from the Romans during the first Jewish revolt (p. 55).

TURIN SHROUD
The Shroud of Turin was long regarded as one of the holiest of Christian relics. It was believed to be the shroud in which Jesus of Nazareth was wrapped following the Crucifixion, and bore an extraordinary image said to be that of Christ himself. Modern scientific testing, using radiocarbon analysis, has since shown that it is in fact a medieval fake.

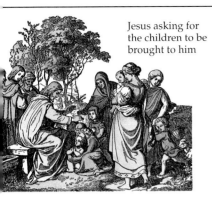

Jesus asking for the children to be brought to him

MOSAIC MAP
In 1884, a remarkable mosaic was discovered in the Greek Orthodox church in Madaba, Jordan. Dating to the 6th century A.D., it depicts a map of the Holy Land with pictures of towns, individual buildings, and other details. Although parts of the map have suffered considerable damage, it preserves a fine illustration of Jerusalem and parts of the Jordan Valley and the Negev.

GOSPEL
This page of St. Luke's Gospel is from a 5th-century text, the Codex Alexandrinus.

ILLUMINATED MANUSCRIPT
In the medieval period, highly decorated or "illuminated" manuscripts of the Bible were produced by monks. This example is from a Latin Bible of around 750, preserved in the Royal Library in Stockholm, Sweden.

BEFORE THE CRUCIFIXION
This portrayal of Christ wearing the crown of thorns is by the 15th-century Flemish painter Quentin Massys.

Continued on next page

Text in Syriac

THE APPEARANCE OF TRANSLATIONS
The Christian church began in the Holy Land and spread through the Mediterranean. When it spread beyond the areas where Greek and Hebrew were spoken, translations into other languages began to appear. As well as Bibles in Latin, Bibles in Egyptian and Syriac appeared. This manuscript of the New Testament was written in 1216 in Syriac.

MOSES AND THE TABLETS
When Moses returned from Mount Sinai he brought with him stone tablets engraved with the law.

Text in Hebrew

SCROLLS OF THE SYNAGOGUE
Hebrew scribes meticulously copied out the texts of the Old Testament books onto parchment, which was rolled up and kept in the Jewish places of worship, the synagogues.

HEBREW BIBLE
This page from a Hebrew Bible shows the story of the Exodus. This is quite a recent Hebrew Bible, but the text has changed very little since the Dead Sea Scrolls were written out almost 2,000 years ago.

Scrolls covered in fine cloth

JESUS IN THE TEMPLE
The young Jesus was once discovered in discussion with the wise men at the Temple. This story shows the importance of scholarship and debate for the Jews – a tradition which has continued to this day. The episode is shown here in a painting by William Holman Hunt (1827-1910).

THE MENORAH

The Hebrew word *menorah* means "lampstand." In the Old Testament it refers specifically to the seven-branched candlestick which stood in the Temple of Jerusalem and later became a Jewish symbol. The menorah was removed from the Temple by the Romans in A.D. 70. It is depicted, with other objects similarly looted, in the carvings on the arch of Titus (p. 55).

THE FIRST PRINTED BIBLE

Johannes Gutenberg was one of the inventors of printing with movable type in the 15th century. His Bible, which appeared in 1456, was the first printed edition. The text was in Latin. Printed texts made the Bible much more accessible. Soon, printed translations of the Bible into the modern European languages started to roll off the press.

Text in Latin

Text in English

KING DAVID

David was the second king of Israel. According to the Bible he began his career as a shepherd boy and was the writer of the Psalms. He is shown here in a painting by Pietro Perugino (1446-1524).

THE BIBLE IN ENGLISH

English translations of the Bible began to appear with a version by John Wycliffe in 1384. William Tyndale was the first English translator to tackle the New Testament. His New Testament first appeared in 1526. It had to be smuggled into England because there was so much opposition to translations of the original biblical texts.

An Arab encampment painted by David Roberts (1796-1864)

Archeology

M ODERN ARCHEOLOGY in the Holy Land began in 1865 with the formation of the Palestine Exploration Fund. The purpose of the fund was to investigate the archeology, geography, geology, and natural history of Palestine. A detailed survey was completed in 1877 and, with accurate maps in hand, archeology could begin. In 1890 the fund engaged British archeologist Flinders Petrie to excavate at Tell el-Hesi. The results were highly influential. Petrie understood exactly what a tell was (pp. 14-15), and developed a system to reveal the complicated series of occupation layers one by one. Petrie established principles still used in archeology today.

W. M. F. PETRIE
Petrie had already made a considerable reputation for himself in Egypt when he was appointed by the Palestine Exploration Fund.

HAND PICK
A small hand pick is ideally suited to the soil conditions in the Holy Land, breaking up the earth cleanly and causing minimal damage to any underlying features or artifacts.

Metal bob hangs vertically

SURVEYOR'S POLE
A ranging pole, 6.5 feet (2 m) long and marked off in red and white 20 in (50 cm) bands, is used not only in surveying but also as a convenient indicator of scale in excavation photographs.

KEEPING VERTICALS VERTICAL
A plumb line is used in planning and making vertical sections. A section through a site is the archeologist's most valuable resource, providing a visual record of the site's sequence of occupation layers.

BETH SHAN
Petrie understood that a tell, like Beth Shan, had formed over generations by the buildup of debris. Archeologists remove the layers one by one, in reverse chronological (time) order. The objects found within each layer are specific to that layer, so studying them shows how the culture of the people changed over the centuries.

GENTLE LEVER *right*
A plasterer's "leaf" is a sensitive tool used for isolating fragile objects from the soil and lifting them up.

GENERAL SIR CHARLES WARREN
Warren investigated Jerusalem on behalf of the Palestine Exploration Fund. The work was very dangerous, involving the sinking of deep shafts, but it provided much information about the construction of the Dome of the Rock (an Islamic shrine built on the site of a Jewish temple) and the platform of Herod's Temple.

TAKING MEASUREMENTS
Precision is essential in archeology. Cloth tapes are used, in conjunction with surveying instruments such as theodolites, to set out the excavation areas and to make accurate plans of excavated features.

TROWELS

These are the standard tools of the archeologist. In the Holy Land trowels are not used much for digging, where their scraping action can cause considerable damage. They are used for cleaning away the soil after it has been broken up with a hand pick and for cutting vertical "section" faces through the soil.

SINAI SURVEYORS

In 1868-1869 the Palestine Exploration Fund mounted an expedition to southern Sinai in order to examine the possible routes of the Exodus. The survey work was carried out by Captain Wilson (shown at the rear smoking a pipe).

SIR CHARLES WILSON

The establishment of the Palestine Exploration Fund was partly inspired by a highly successful survey of Jerusalem undertaken in 1864 by Wilson and a team of Royal Engineers from the British Army.

CARRY-ALL

For work in the field some sort of site bag is essential for carrying equipment – notebooks, pens, tape measure, nails, string, labels, bags for finds, and countless other items.

Strap fits around waist

HANDY RULER

Small 6-ft (2-m) or 9-ft (3-m) tape measures are invaluable for planning, section drawing, and measuring excavated features and objects.

Index

Acknowledgments

Dorling Kindersley would like to thank:
Jacquie Gulliver for help with the initial stages of the book; Céline Carez, Bernadette Crowley, and Claire Gillard for editorial assistance; Liz Sephton for design assistance; Jane Parker for the index; Lisa Bliss, Kevin Lovelock, and John Williams of the British Museum for additional photography; Peter Akkermans, Samantha Bolden, Rupert L. Chapman, Peter Dorrell, Peter Rea, Dianne Rowan, and Kathryn W. Tubb for further assitance.

Maps Eugene Fleury
Models David Donkin

Picture credits

t=top, b=bottom, c=center, l=left, r=right

J. C. Allen: 7b, 23cb, 59tr.
Ancient Art & Architecture Collection: 43tl, 61tl.
Ashmolean Museum, Oxford: 38c.
Werner Braun: 6b, 27tl, 57cr.
Birmingham Museum and Art Galleries: 60b.
Bridgeman Art Library: 50br detail, 57tr detail; /AtkinsonArt Gallery, Southport 61b; Bible Society, London 58cr, 59cl, 60tl, 61cr; /Christies, London 38bl, 61cl; /Gavin Graham Gallery, London 32cl detail; /Guildhall Library 12b, 42c detail; /Musée des Beaux-Arts, Nantes 61tr; /Prado, Madrid 59bc; /Private Collection 28tr, 60cr; /Royal Library Stockholm 59cr; /Victoria & Albert Museum, London 30tr detail.

Trustees of the British Museum, London: 8bl, 15tr, 18bl, 19b, 42cr.
Dr. P. Dorrell, Institute of Archaeology: 8cr.
Egyptian Museum, Cairo: 20c.
E. T. Archive, Victoria & Albert Museum: 7tl.
Mary Evans Picture Library: 21br, 26tl, 41cr, 44tr.
Giraudon Louvre: 41tl.
Sonia Halliday Photographs: 6tl, 6cl, 14bl, 43c, 55tc, 62c.
Hamburger Kunsthalle: 34br detail, 46tl detail.
Robert Harding Picture Library: 10cl, 49br, 52bl, 58cl.
Michael Holford: 22-23b, 28tl, 35cl, 38, 41cl, 46-7.
Dept. of Antiquities, Israel Museum: front jacket cl, 17t, 24bl, 35bc, 43tr, 58cl.
Kobal Collection: 37c.
Kunsthistorisches Museum, Vienna: 10–11b.

Mansell Collection: 59tl.
National Gallery, London: 30br detail, 55cl detail.
National Maritime Museum, Haifa: 40-41b.
Palestine Exploration Fund: 62tl, 62bl, 63tl, 63tr.
Zev Radovan: 6cb, 13cl, 15tl, 15cl, 17cr, 27tr, 57c;/ Scala: 55tl.
Jamie Simpson: 12c.
Sotheby's, London: 7tr.
Amoret Tanner: front jacket tl, back jacket bl, 12tl, 28cb, 29tl, 29bc, 32tr, 33br.
Victoria & Albert Museum: 59bl.
Zefa; 7c, 50bl.